I0210414

By Fowlers Fork

poems by

Chuck Stringer

Finishing Line Press
Georgetown, Kentucky

By Fowlers Fork

for Susan

ACKNOWLEDGMENTS

My thanks to the editors of the literary journals in which earlier versions of
these poems have appeared:

Anthropocene: Poems About Environment: "What's Coming"
For a Better World : "Black Lives Matter"
Pine Mountain Sand & Gravel: "Poem for the Pandemic;" "Time Machine;"
"This Year;" "Coyote"
Riparian: "shift"
Words: "Pantoum, in which we stop to sit"

The poems in this collection have been inspired and nourished by the
community of poets gathering in the classes, workshops, and retreats offered
by our teachers and mentors: Pauletta Hansel, Sherry Cook Stanforth, and
Richard Hague. My deepest gratitude to you all.

And a special thank you to my fellow creek walkers, artist Michael DeMaria
and photographer Alison Ford, for their creative contributions.

Publisher: Leah Huete de Maines
Editor: Christen Kincaid
Cover Art: Michael DeMaria
Author Photos: Alison Ford
Cover Design: Elizabeth Maines McCleavy

Order online: www.finishinglinepress.com
also available on amazon.com

Author inquiries and mail orders:
Finishing Line Press
PO Box 1626
Georgetown, Kentucky 40324
USA

Table of Contents

There are no unsacred places;
there are only sacred places
and desecrated places.
>> —Wendell Berry, "How to Be a Poet"

You will show me the path of life;
in your presence there is fullness of joy,
and in your right hand are pleasures for evermore.
>> —Psalm16:11

This Year

Do not be afraid—I will save you.
I have called you by name—you are mine.
—Isaiah 43:1

Today I wake dreaming
of sparrows. I'd dreamed them
through the redbud and black
walnut out by Second Bridge,
and they'd each shared
their singular songs: chipping,
swamp, white-crowned,
American tree. I lie here
in bed awhile with Memory
and listen, then we walk
back to a June afternoon below
Two-Stair Crossing to watch
a bird with a brown-streaked
belly hop from rock to rock
bobbing its tail and snatching
gnats. Louisiana waterthrush.
Yes, I reach out to Memory
to relive that chance encounter—
one bird, one man, and less than
five grand minutes connected
by the creek. We walk a little
farther downstream where
a rush of July and August
friends fly in to greet us: ducks,
herons, woodpeckers, wood-
warblers, mimics, and jays.

Sitting up, but not
quite out of bed, I'm ready
to pull on my Mucks,
put on my mask, pick up
my walking stick and head
for the creek hopeful
that, with distance and luck,
I'll keep hearing the name
Chuck this year.

Gift

Grateful to be retired when you rise; to not set an alarm,
sit in traffic, run meetings, fight deadlines, answer
to a boss; to possess every day your own space and time;
to have a table and a chair on a back porch near
sycamores, with a cat lying on a rail, and a laptop next
to your toast and tea; to write as you watch birds gather
at your feeders—vessels like a self filled with gift—
suet, cracked corn, sunflower seed; to know there's a path
along a creek close by you will walk in a couple of hours
like an Adam walking in the Garden with God, naming
each creature, doing no harm; to come home to a partner
of forty-nine years who sits in a favorite chair, reading;
to watch as she plucks and tastes like a second Eve
the crisp unruffled pages of another great mystery.

Velocity

...the rate of change of displacement with time.
—physics.info/velocity

An unexpected green scurries and hides beneath edges in a wash. Just a bug. But, oh, what a green gleaming in the sun, iridescent and metallic. I transfer my catch to a lidded empty bottle I keep in my pack. At home I google "green bugs" and determine it's a beetle, emerald ash borer, native to Asia, transported to America. Here no jewel but invasive killer of white, black, green, and blue ash. Seven years for larvae to murder their way south from Michigan to Kentucky. And having found and named a terrible beauty, but being no god, I carry it with haste back to the creek, watch it scurry its green across the wash.

Marlboro Man

It's a little anonymous game we play each week on the trails
by the creek. He and his black Great Dane must see me

picking up trash, but it doesn't keep him from flicking
wrappers and butts everywhere. I low-mutter

"Marlboro Man" then bend to bag his careless toss
in a pool where silted bedrock calls to crayfish.

They dart and back away from the empty pack
of Gold's as if to shout out a complaint,

"Don't break the spell of wildness!" I curse
him again with the name, watch gold-

striped cellophane drop and settle under
Conversation Falls. Still, I guess

I should thank him now and again
for providing the constant

means to serve humble
a little closer to

earth.

morning mist apocalypse

crows
at the end
of each dead branch

shadow smoke

high as
this white oak
goes

Time Machine

Today, picking up a knapped chert flake
I see South Fork's hand of flowing mystery
has set back the dial on the creek wash
one thousand years. And though I've walked
this way before, it takes a one-inch midnight
rain to make a muddy flake flash its name
in August daylight. I listen to a field sparrow
singing in the distance, like the man who once
crouched here listened over each loud crack
when again and again he struck a sediment's
hard fist with his hammer stone. A few steps
later, a fossil brachiopod, perfectly preserved
and waiting—just as it waited on the bottom
of a sea—waiting for me four hundred million
years to come, pick it up, hold it with the chert
and revel in the time together we travel.

Question for a Sycamore

Did your falling
   bark like a scroll
unravel any dark
      tree meaning?

Below

Early morning crossing Second Bridge another round of late-night graffiti. Wildness sprayed with a fluorescent blue paint. **DUMB COON** in caps on the south end. Dead center a pair of disembodied balls— Klee-like spheres with faces that ghost the concrete. Almost touching them **conners mom is sexy** inscribed in lower case. Out beyond the guardrail something darts and hovers darts and hovers in the creek below. I turn and wind on Orleans Trail toward Chinkapin Run but slow to tread a twenty-foot penis spurting **BDE. Bitch pis** blues the blacktop followed by **Fuck 12 FUCK BLM** and the neatly spaced letters **N i g g e r**. A few more feet and there's a wispy smudge telling me here they ran out of paint. A crumpled can sits on the bank above Third Bridge Wash where tomorrow I'll probably see my friend on the grounds crew. But this time he can't scrub the paint away. This time it will have to be covered. And when he's done, the syrupy tar will dry to an ugly scar to remind us darkness darts and hovers darts and hovers.

Black Lives Matter

Even combing the bottom
of the creek for artifacts,
debris I find reminders
of the sickness: a tile shard
stamped with the words MADE IN US—
the A like America
having been broken away.

Poem for the Pandemic, March 18, 2020

Tonight the creek
is raging. As I cross
the bridge on Fowlers Fork
I wonder if it too
will succumb
and go under. All day
this valley has been filling
with rain, the right
and left banks
humbled. Roiling water
slaps the edges
by my feet and many
of my markers
will be swept away. Now
it's easy to see
what the map
with a phantom
dotted line attempts
to define. And like
the flood zone raging
it comes to me—
This is why this place
stays wild.

shift

within

the still
beyond

the flow
watch

an upside down
forest

in the creek
mirror

grow

grow

mirror
in the creek

forest
an upside down

watch
the flow

beyond
the still

within

Coyote

The first coyote I ever saw here was sitting by the bridge twenty years ago as I slowed on Mount Zion Road to make a left on Gunpowder. It looked at me like it owned the place and I guess it did. On my return twenty minutes later it wasn't there. And I think I heard one late a summer's evening standing on my back porch at new moon to look at the stars. A low-toned primal growl stirred something dark in my body, something *coyote*, something mostly forgotten but a little too familiar. The only other one I've seen was running fast down a left-bank ridge chasing a cottontail. I had stopped in the middle of Fowlers Fork when the rabbit jumped the tall bank and brushed by my boots like a hard-tossed stone skipped across the creek. I got worried when the coyote kept on coming, when it stopped at the edge of a limestone ledge above me. Close up, streaks of auburn, fire in eyes. We stared at each other for a long time with a wary start and tug of recognition, then it turned and disappeared. That was last year, and since only a highway of tracks in mud and ice and snow. But I know the coyote are there. Wildness lurking at the edges, waiting, watching.

Lunation's Refrain

For more than twelve months a year
this lunar mystery
      brims,
        dim darkness to light to darkness dim;

as moon, with earth and sun,
in gravity's tidal pool
      swims,
        dim darkness to light to darkness dim;

or a newborn unlocks night to wax
its days till the reaper
      trims,
        dim darkness to light to darkness dim;

sing praise, for another sun's coming
ends the cycle sky
      hymns,
        dim darkness to light to darkness dim.

These Tracks Like Hieroglyphs

What charm
or curse
has a stalking heron left
in this mud-encrusted
stone?

in a month with little rain

in a month with little rain
  soles tread the trickle's footsteps
                hidden spring offerings bubble up & pool
    water spiders tap dance the tips of bedrock

in a month with little rain
            minnows teem & dart in murky puddles
  deer walk a trail down limestone's lowest road
              water snakes wind & slip into crevices

in a month with little rain
  orange in jewelweed droops like shriveled cradles
              mud-caked shards bake in the wash
    the creek sits in silence with its ten thousand stones

in a month with little rain
    each thirsty day questions & stares, hot & weary
  debris still hangs in the August-flooded trees
            & Fowlers Fork shows its long-buried bones

What's Coming

*Climate projections for the late 21st century have
suggested that the conditions favorable for the
development of the severe storms that produce
tornadoes will increase over North America, and
the impact could be greatest in the winter and fall.*
—John T. Allen, *USA Today, Dec. 13, 2021*

Outlier? We can hope so, though like a family that
survived but now lives in the rubble and chaos of
Mayfield we ask ourselves, "Is this the new normal?"
Walking by the creek it's an even sixty degrees in the
middle of December. Climate change is on my mind—
mind can't let it go. Images of Hiroshima houses,
stripped and mutilated trees, a flattened factory. Layer
on layer of paper, plastic, plywood, metal, concrete.
Cruel this stratum of graffiti, torn and tortured skin
that held (and still may hold) the dead. Even so, we shy
away from any change, bitch about the high price of gas
then drop $50K to purchase a loaded Dodge Ram that
won't get fifteen mpg charging down a city street. And
high on most people's list a good cut of beef, heavy on
the hoof and carbon footprint. We eat what we will,
caring not as an ark load of NOAA forecasters code
the next showstopper. Meanwhile, Carolina wrens
chirp from a barren hickory. Fox squirrels daredevil
down to earth untethered, crisscross rusty leaves in
search of hoarded nuts instinct buried for winter.
Right now, to them, is all that's real. And I wonder,
"Do they know what's coming, *may be already here?*"

Heal-all

Mid-July, time of hot sun, pink
and white phlox, humidity, thunderstorm.
Heavy rain has ceased
for an hour, but Fowlers Fork is still rising
against my Mucks. Magic of evening
upstream summer daylight, flow.
On the left bank your purple cap, wildness come
to greet me, like the mosquitoes landing silent on my arm.
Raindrops ripple in the creek before I feel them.

Last Bloom

At noon a sudden joy to see your face shining in the field. Chicory in the grasses all summer long, I thought you had died and gone. Greens, yellows mingle in box elders, elms, and every sycamore browns its leaves. They'll pile and turn to rust in matted, soggy puddles—loss like an unsaid prayer. But today I find you praying.

Pantoum, in which we stop to sit

beside the creek. Only you and I
to ponder it. I walk with the one who makes me,
who knows the reasons why.
The creek flows on, a mystery.

Ponder it: I walk with a power who breaks me.
Wildness leads to a cold, hard rain.
The creek flows on—a mystery
that we sometimes walk in pain.

Wildness. Cold, hard rain.
No movement on the bank. No movement in the trees.
That we sometimes walk in pain
a blessing you give that frees.

Movement on a bank, movement in a tree
beside the creek only you and I,
these blessings you give that free.
Who knows the reasons why?

aging poet

catbird skulks
a thicket of dying
green

gray shadow

known this evening
by its quiet
mews

Elegy

The average life expectancy of a butterfly
is typically about three to four weeks...
—butterflyidentification.com

Thankful for another year
to walk this wash, where last month
a pearl crescent circled
seven times, landed on stone, spread
black and orange wings
for a few fateful seconds, lifted
then fluttered into this poem.

With You

I walk the wildness
on this trail,
then find a voice
& calling, say aloud
each name: mink,
beaver, muskrat,
chipmunk, gray
squirrel, raccoon,
opossum & white-
tailed deer;
shagbark hickory,
Chinkapin oak,
American hornbeam
& osage orange;
black-eyed Susan,
moneywort,
white snakeroot &
yellow foxtail;
green heron, belted
kingfisher,
eastern wood-
peewee, red-bellied
woodpecker, great
horned owl,
turkey vulture,
mallard, red-tailed
& red-shouldered
hawk; eastern tiger
swallowtail,

monarch, gnat &
horse-fly; wolf
spider; hellbender,
American bullfrog
& American toad;
snapping turtle;
crayfish; creek chub
& pumpkinseed.
How many more
yet to be found &
named.

Sunday

A new place, just below West Bend, on a slanted
limestone slab tossed into Fowlers Fork only God knows
how long ago. Left stands a black oak. Right arcs
a sugar maple's upturned trunk. Trees charged
with curling brown and yellow leaves all clinging, dying.
Get comfortable. Bend knees, seat butt, rest boots
on the creek bottom. Water laps a stack of broken stone. One leaf
breaks free, falls, hits the surface, then makes it way
past a honey locust because something besides gravity
keeps on pulling it downstream where you will be headed
when you stand, take up your walking stick, *go*.

After a Hard Rain on Monday

and another day to let a muddy creek clear, how did I know
the light would be right this evening? New chert

shards appear in the sands and gravels washed by Fowlers Fork
flow. And for any persistent enough to walk it day by day

upstream and down, even sometimes like tonight by the light
of a setting sun, the telltale shape of a perfect point. I'm lucky

once, maybe twice a year. Tough odds. But the thrill of it—
to see and retrieve and hold *whole* what a Fort Ancient hunter

made and launched and lost. So I keep on coming back
sometimes getting lucky like tonight by the light of a setting sun.

three wishes

to be blue
like a bunting, perch in a tree
and sing, look out
                      & fly away

Notes on Selected Poems:

The poems in this chapbook were inspired by my almost daily walks along the deer paths on the last mile of Fowlers Fork, a creek in the Gunpowder Watershed, located in Boone County, Kentucky. Most of the place names that appear in the poems are my own.

This Year

"Mucks": Muck boots

Velocity

The invasive emerald ash borer "was first identified in Canton, Michigan (near Detroit) in 2002" (*Wikipedia*). In 2009 it was identified in Kentucky.

Below

"Orleans Trail": a City of Florence paved pedestrian walkway

"BDE": "Big dick energy" (urbandictionary.com)

"Bitch pis": "a girl's drink" (urbandictionary.com)

"Fuck 12": "Fuck 12" basically means fuck the police" (urbandictionary.com)

I spell out the N-word (I will not utter it) in this poem with great reluctance, and only after consulting my African-American son-in-law Nigel who advised me, "This word needs to stay in this poem, needs to be called out and named." Five years ago, my then eleven-year-old African-American grandson Shaun had asked, "Grandad, why do people hate me?" My tearful response about thirty seconds later was "I don't know, Shaun. I don't know."

What's Coming

"During the late evening of Friday, December 10, 2021, a violent, long-tracked tornado moved across Western Kentucky, producing severe to catastrophic damage in numerous towns, including Mayfield" (*Wikipedia*).

Chuck Stringer has spent a lifetime roaming woods, rivers, and creeks—first in New England, then in East Tennessee, and for the last forty-five years in Kentucky. He worked at Johnson Controls, Inc. in Warehousing and Distribution Management for more than thirty-three years. He has a BA degree in English from Carson-Newman University and has completed graduate courses in creative writing at the University of Cincinnati, with further studies at Northern Kentucky University and Thomas More University. Since retiring in 2013, he has been blessed to be a part of the community of regional poets writing in the classes, workshops, and retreats offered by Cincinnati-area poets and teachers Pauletta Hansel, Sherry Cook Stanforth, and Richard Hague.

In September of 2016 he and wife Susan moved to their home on a ridge above Fowlers Fork in Boone County, Kentucky. He works with the city of Florence to clean and maintain its last mile, trying to live by his creekkeeper's motto: "Every time I walk this way/I try to leave it a little wilder."

Chuck is a member of the Southern Appalachian Writers Cooperative. His poems have been published in *Anthropocene: Poems About Environment, For a Better World, Literary Accents, Pine Mountain Sand & Gravel, Riparian*, and other journals.

This is his first collection.

www.ingramcontent.com/pod-product-compliance
Lightning Source LLC
Chambersburg PA
CBHW022051080426
42734CB00009B/1296